BOOK OF TYPES AND TYPE MATERIAL

BOOK OF TYPES
AND TYPE MATERIAL

AS USED AT THE PRINTING PRESS OF
WILKES & CO LTD, LONDON

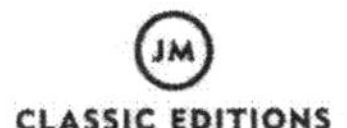

CLASSIC EDITIONS

INDEX

PAGE

5 Erbar Light Grot.

6 Erbar Medium Grot.

7 **Erbar Bold Grot.**

8 Bernhard Roman

8 *Bernhard Italic*

9 *Bernhard Cursive*

10 *Bernhard Roman, Italic and Cursive Ornaments*

11 *Bernhard Cursive Bold*

12 **Bernhard Roman Bold**

13 Plantin Mono

14 MODERN ROMAN

14 *MODERN ITALIC*

14 OLD STYLE ROMAN

14 *OLD STYLE ITALIC*

15 Tiemann Old Style

16 **Goudy Bold**

17 ***Goudy Bold Italic***

18 *Goudy Italic*

18 *Clear Face Italic*

19 **Cooper Black**

20 ***Cooper Black Ital.***

21 Bodoni Light

PAGE

22 Bodoni Medium

23 **Bodoni Bold**

24 **Ultra Bodoni**

25 **Nubian**

26 **NEULAND**

27 Narciss

28 **MAXIMILIAN**

28 *FOURNIER*

29 *Bulletin*

29 *Charcoal*

30 ***Samson***

31 Scotch Roman

32 *Scotch Roman Italic*

32 ***Plymouth Italic***

33 *Bodoni Medium Italic*

33 *Old Face Italic*

34 Old Face

35 **Old Face Heavy**

36 BOOKLET

36 Garamond

37 *Garamond Italic*

INDEX

PAGE

37 *Cloister Bold Italic*

38 Cochin

39 *Cochin Italic*

40 **Cochin Bold**

41 Plantin

42 *Plantin Italic*

43 VESTA

44 Hallamshire

44 Kennerley

45 Cheltenham Wide

45 Gloucester

46 **Gloucester Bold**

46 **Cheltenham Bold**

47 ***Chelt. Bold Italic***

47 *Cheltenham Italic*

47 *Gloucester Italic*

48 **Cheltenham Bold Con.**

49 **Chelt. Bold Ex.**

50 Chelt. Inline

50 Chelt. In. Con.

51 Chelt. Bold Shaded

52 **John Hancock**

53 **John Hancock Con.**

PAGE

54 **Roycroft**

54 Roycroft Open

55 **Adtype**

56 Westminster

56 Cochin Open

57 Wren

57 **Comstock**

58 & 59   TYPEWRITER

60 SPARTAN

60 **COPPERPLATE**

61 **Heavy Grot.**

61 Light Grot.

62 Bartlett

63 Author's Roman

64 Cushing

64 **Gothic**

65 Flemish Black

66 Abbey Text

67 INITIALS

68 to 79   BORDERS

80 & 81   RULES

82 & 83   Advertising Brackets

ERBAR LIGHT GROT.

72 Point — Caps only

ABOUT THIS

54 Point — Caps only

TIME (1927) NO

30 Point

VERY WONDERFUL OR
commendable recordings

24 Point

IT IS NOT GIVEN TO ALL OF US
to wander in search of the world's

18 Point

SOME OF US HAVE THE OPPORTUNITY,
most of us have not. Many, no doubt, if
it was possible, would consider the best

14 Point

SOME EVEN ARE SO
fortunate as to live in a
country possessing a great

12 Point

FEW OF US OURSELVES
possess great works of art, and
therefore very few can hope to
secure and retain more than

10 Point

DOES ANY ONE OF US FAIL TO
derive some pleasure from the work
of a great artist? How many of us
envy the artist his gift in being able

8 Point

YET EACH ONE OF US, IF WE DID BUT
realize it can contribute to the art of the
world. Each can give something of beauty
that others may look upon, something
that for years after will retain its original

ERBAR MEDIUM GROT.

72 Point

IN QUITE A considerable

54 Point

FOR OVER 68 years it has been

42 Point

NEARLY everyone

30 Point

RESEARCH enables the

24 Point

INNUMERABLE instances can be

18 Point

COMPREHENSIVE as these initial stages

14 Point

EXCEPTIONALLY LARGE and spontaneous were the

12 Point

IT ALSO PRODUCES A VAST element which, although considered basically sound, must

10 Point

CHARACTERISTIC IN ALL THESE details, it is surprising, considering the colossal and instantaneous effect

8 Point

SIMPLE THINGS, IF THEY POSSESS A splendid merit, usually capture the imagination in preference to the complex. The effectiveness of the most elaborate

ERBAR BOLD GROT.

72 Point

TO DERIVE
satisfactory

54 Point

ALTOGETHER
there are 150

42 Point

TRYING
as these

30 Point

TO FULLY
realize the

24 Point

MORE THAN
the usual time

18 Point

A CONSIDERABLE
quantity should be

14 Point

ELECTRIC CURRENT IS
generated through an

12 Point

IT REPRESENTS THE RATE
of current flow necessary to
overcome the resistance of

10 Point

WHERE NO PROVISION IS MADE
to reverse every alternate flow
of current, and here it would be

8 Point

IN THE UTILISATION OF FRICTIONAL
electricity, its distribution over a surface
conductor has to be provided for, and
although in some cases it has not been

BERNHARD ROMAN and BERNHARD ROMAN ITALIC

48 Point Bernhard Roman

A FINE
and really

36 Point

WHEN A
contrast has

30 Point

THE TRUE
principle for the

24 Point

GARDENING
is one of the most

18 Point

IT WAS ABOUT
the year 1925 that better

14 Point

MOREOVER, IN SPITE
of all the modern facilities for

12 Point

IT MAY BE TAKEN AS
an incontrovertible fact that the
delicacy, freshness and perfection

36 Point Bernhard Roman Italic

ROUND
about 1928

30 Point

TALL AND
graceful, such a

24 Point

FOR PLANTS
that have yielded a
perfect and natural

18 Point

MANY FAILURES
in growing can be traced
to planting varieties that
are self-sterile; to those

14 Point

THE ROCKERY, OR
Rock Garden, be it large or
small, is generally a matter of
individual taste and utilisation
of opportunity in the choice

12 Point

CHRYSANTHEMUM
culture has made remarkable head-
way in recent years. With petals
fantastically curled and twisted,
these flowers may often be reared
under conditions that would have

BERNHARD CURSIVE

54 Point

A B C D

The touch is dainty, delicate and precise, for

36 Point

E F G H I J K

In design and construction, the two vital problems are solved. Since 1926

24 Point

L M N O P Q R

Their general perfection has maintained for them a place of their very own in the forefront of the musical world. Resonance is perfect, embodying

18 Point

S T U V W X Y Z

Its refined appearance harmonises entirely with all the surroundings, and forms, with the cachet and distinction that its finish embodies, all the qualities of a first = class

BERNHARD CURSIVE BOLD

72 Point

A B C

Here are unique

54 Point

D E F G

Picturesque scenes are

42 Point

H I J K L

A typical grandeur that is

36 Point

M N O P Q R

To fully appreciate this exquisite

30 Point

S T U

The delicacy and

24 Point

V W X Y Z

Artistic and modern

18 Point

Rare and distinctive
edifices characterize the
1   2   3   4   5

14 Point

Fine views are a feature, the
roads prolific in panoramas.
Innumerable and resplendent

BERNHARD ROMAN BOLD

24 Point

POPULARITY
distinguished the
1 2 3 4 5 6

20 Point

THE METHOD
of exposition of the
demonstration here

18 Point

YET FOR THESE
very reasons the piece
forms a capital and
natural introduction to

14 Point

THE MASTERLY WAY
in which the Composer has
contrasted and related this
material, and the way in
which out of it he has been

12 Point

IT WOULD SEEM THAT
a Capriccio should naturally
be capricious, but this one is
quite orderly. Yet it is very
jolly and full of life. To fully
appreciate the merits of this

10 Point

THERE IS INSPIRATION IN
a fine piece of music, but there is
also craftsmanship. Incidentally,
the enjoyment of craftsmanship is
a part of the enjoyment of art,
as you may learn from the chance
conversation of any connoisseur of

72 Point

FOR
those

60 Point

NOR
should

48 Point

QUITE
24 kinds

36 Point

RECENT
artistic and

30 Point

SKILFULLY
arranged, this

PLANTIN MONO and ITALIC

12 Point

Light is, of course, at its best at midday, and very much better in summer than in winter. The quickest exposures are possible at midday in June and longer exposures become

In early morning and late afternoon the exposures must be lengthened, even when the light otherwise is good. The subject itself influences the time of exposure very much, and

ABCDEFGHIJKLMNOPQRSTUVWXYZ

ABCDEFGHIJKLMNOPQRSTUVWXYZ

£1234567890

11 Point

Most portrait negatives are improved by a little retouching. The work is not difficult if one employs the proper materials and goes the right way to work. The necessary materials are now put up in

The secret of successful retouching is to use a lead pencil with a point as sharp as a needle, so at to put on as little lead as will give the required effect and in the right place. The whole of the face is not

ABCDEFGHIJKLMNOPQRSTUVWXYZ

ABCDEFGHIJKLMNOPQRSTUVWXYZ

£1234567890

10 Point

Many negatives that are faulty because of errors made in exposure and development, may be considerably improved by the application of certain chemicals. If, however, you use gaslight paper for printing, there is very often no need to " improve " a defective negative, because this paper

Negatives fit to intensify must be free from fog, full of detail, but weak in density—the kind of negative produced by correct exposure and under-development. Remember that an intensifier cannot increase details, all it will do is to strengthen them ; they must be in the negative to start with.

ABCDEFGHIJKLMNOPQRSTUVWXYZ

ABCDEFGHIJKLMNOPQRSTUVWXYZ

£1234567890

8 Point

The advantages that the Reflex camera places in the hands of most workers are very obvious. First and foremost the camera, although no larger than an ordinary small hand-camera, enables the worker who is an indifferent judge of distance to depend upon getting his pictures accurately composed and perfectly

Although admirably fitted for every kind of photographic work, including portraiture, copying and architectural photography, it is particularly in instantaneous photography that this form of camera is pre-eminent. Fitted as it is with a focal-plane shutter giving a great range of speeds, there is practically no subject in

ABCDEFGHIJKLMONPQRSTUVWXYZ

ABCDEFGHIJKLMNOPQRSTUVWXYZ

£1234567890

The above series available in 14, 18, 24, 30 and 36 point

MODERN and MODERN ITALIC
OLD STYLE and OLD STYLE ITALIC

12 Point Lining Modern

COPY & CIRCULATION.
Advertising consists of two
things, copy and circulation.
Copy includes all that has

10 Point Mono Modern

TOO MUCH MONEY IS SPENT
in advertising — also not enough.
Too much power is attributed to
advertising—also not enough. The
thing is out of balance and will

8 Point

RESEARCH IS A PART OF COPY.
Knowledge of the product is a part. An
understanding of the present existing
merchandising methods, service policies,
volume of sales, field of operations,
present and prospective customers, the

6 Point

COPY IS THE STORY OF THE BUSINESS,
and it must be a true story, interestingly told,
or its circulation will be of small avail. When
the copy is as nearly right as we can make it,
we are ready to buy circulation. We want
enough circulation, but not too much — and
we want the right kind, which, in local retail

5 Point Lining Modern

QUITE RECENTLY WE HAD THE OPPORTUNITY
to compare the advertising activities of several big
concerns in different cities. In many cases the per-
centage paid for advertising did not compare very
favourably with the returns. Sound business calls
occasionally for a reduction, and this can be made
in two ways: (1) by an actual curtailment of the
expenditure, (2) by improving the effectiveness of

12 Point Lining Modern Italic

*NO MATTER WHAT
the form of advertising, in
no matter what business,*

10 Point Mono Modern Italic

*TOO OFTEN, ADVERTISING
is expected to offset, counteract, and
overbalance, weaknesses and errors
in product, price, and organization.*

8 Point

*IN RETAIL ADVERTISING, THIS
fact is more direct and obvious, and therefore retail advertising problems are comparatively simple, but nevertheless, the
principles used in successful advertising*

6 Point

*IN NEARLY EVERY CASE, ANALYSIS
disclosing the facts and figures of the business
and its field, and their relation to each other,
will point unerringly to the kind and amount of
the advertising which should be done. The element
of gamble cannot be eliminated, but it can be*

10 Point Lining Old Style

THE PURPOSE & INTENT
of all business men is to make
money. To make money they
must sell goods. If advertising
is to be of use to business men,
it must sell or help directly to
sell goods. If, then, that is its
purpose, why not call it written
or printed or published salesmanship? Only those sales constitute

8 Point

THE LARGER ADVERTISERS ARE
realizing more than ever that copy is
one of their real problems. They have
developed their products, their methods
of distribution, and their sales forces
to a high point of efficiency. They,
for the most part, know where and
when to advertise. The weak link—
if there is a weak link—is copy. Once
found, the right copy may effect sales
and profits to a greater degree than
anything else. That is why infinitely

6 Point

CAN THE PRINTER SELL SOMETHING
more than paper, ink, composition, and press-
work? Is it possible to force printing to
produce additional sales for the merchant who
will take sound advice on how it can be made
to do so? Can the printer sell such business
compelling printing? Can he add that force
which is not paper, ink, composition, or press-
work to make printing profitable? The answer
is Yes. It is being done every day, and doing
it is the simplest kind of plain common sense.
Some perhaps do it better than others, some
worse. In an address made at a recent con-
vention, a speaker told of a printer who, with

10 Point Lining Old Style Italic

*THERE IS NOT A SOUND
business concern which would
not be benefited by the aid of
Printed Salesmanship. Most of
them sell in "class" markets—
railroads, contracting firms, re-
tailers, and so on — and want
to know how to reach these
markets without the enormous
expenditures called for by the*

6 Point

*IT HAS OFTEN BEEN URGED THAT
an article that is largely advertised must
be costly. Well, those who affirm such a
thing know nothing about it, and certainly
cannot have given the subject any serious
thought, for the reverse is entirely the
case. Their argument could only hold good
if advertising produced no extra demand
for an advertised article; and who would
advertise at all if that were the case?
It is one of the leading factors in the
economics of advertising, that successful
advertising means such an increase of
sales as not only enables production to*

16 Point

FACTS, REASONS &
Ideas dominate every
business, and soon all
the properties that go

14 Point

DESIRE, AND FACTS,
Reasons and Ideas are, to
some extent, the vehicles
upon which the particular
business must certainly be

12 Point

WITHOUT THOSE, THE
Business would be as dead to
desire as mankind would be
to sound, if air, the medium
that carries it, were destroyed.
Then again we must be able

10 Point

THE POLICY? IT IS THIS!
Let us view it with the correct
mental attitude. The policy that
prompts the manufacturer to
advertise to a buyer is basically
sound. It also produces a very
great element as regards what

8 Point

THE SUCCESS OF "ADVERTISING"
depends upon (1) What is said in the
message; (2) How it is duplicated;
(3) How it is carried to those who
read it; (4) What readers it is carried
to. These things influence advertising
to a great extent, and it is only by
employing such methods that it is

6 Point

TIME & EDUCATION WILL TAKE CARE
of such conditions, and eventually we shall
learn to face the facts. Meanwhile, we make
our bow and our exit, gracefully we trust,
but with a sure sense of conscious rectitude,
hoping that the deductions and conclusions
that have been mentioned will be shared
by the many whose interests and ideas tend
toward the benefits each and every one of

48 Point

TACT
factors

36 Point

FANCY
imagined

30 Point

JUSTIFIES
everything?

24 Point

DOMINATES
conservatively
almost all those

18 Point

MANUFACTURER
Manufacturers often
have to prepare for
the huge sales that
take place during a

GOUDY BOLD

18 Point

PERMANENCY
and dignity were
considered when
designing many
of these unique

14 Point

EMBOSSING WITH
acid often produces
the desired effect, as
different textures can
be obtained either by
the use of different
strengths — which on

12 Point

GRANITE, WHICH IS
the hardest of all stones,
is quite impervious to the
effects of weather, and
takes a high, enduring
polish. The picturesque
emerald pearl variety has
the advantage of being
easily distinguishable, for

10 Point

WITHIN RECENT YEARS,
the jet black variety has been
more generally employed and
has gained favour especially
where high class work has to
be maintained. Pilaster bases
are invariably cast in granite,
whatever the composition of
the entablature or upper part.
It is a matter of very great
importance that only the best

60 Point

ONE
often

48 Point

NINE
bronze

36 Point

WHITE
marble is

30 Point

IN 1928 A
scheme for
beautifying

24 Point

OVER AND
over again it
attained quite

72 Point

DURING those very

36 Point

EXACTING AND arduous times were

24 Point

THE FLEXIBILITY AND snappiness that characterized

18 Point

WHATEVER MAY HAVE BEEN the practice hitherto, it should not be forgotten that in dealing with all the

14 Point

A PROSPEROUS BUSINESS MUST HAVE for its foundation an ever increasing number of satisfied customers. Incalculable harm inevitably

12 Point

IT IS BECAUSE SUCH ideals dominate that often an achievement is recorded that seemed during initial

10 Point

IT HAS BEEN NOTICED that in every case where the technical side has been entirely mastered, the ultimate result of undertakings necessitating

CLEAR FACE BOLD ITALIC and GOUDY ITALIC

36 Point Clear Face Bold Italic

THERE is first & foremost

48 Point Goudy Italic

GEMS rare &

30 Point

THE TOP portion is fitted with a 1st class

36 Point

IT IS AS easy and restful as

24 Point

THIS IS AN ideal & also a handsome design, made after the style

30 Point

QUALITY and prices are still the

18 Point

A LUXURIOUS lounge, built on a foundation of resilient springs. This is indeed an inexpensive and

24 Point

THE PRICE quoted is for the 1st & 2nd

18 Point

A VERY NEAT settee consisting of a wire spring mattress and very

COOPER BLACK

30 Point

SYSTEM & ideas

24 Point

NOTICE! remember

18 Point

CO-PARTNER 1st, 4th & 6th

14 Point

THE CONDITIONS still remain, and are likely to keep

12 Point

THE METROPOLITAN and also the General Omnibus Company are

10 Point

REMEMBER! SUCCESS in any line depends upon the use of constructive arguments based upon a

8 Point

SELL WITH FACTS. GOOD AND well-thought-out copy refrains from disparagement of a competitors products or selling policy. This cannot be the same

6 Point

SIMPLICITY IS A COMMENDABLE quality, whether it be in eating, in dress, in beauty, or even in dealing with problems. Every one no doubt has at some time or other been confronted by a problem which has placed them in a quandary. If the policy of this simple idea should be

72 Point

SIT fire

60 Point

FUN joke

48 Point

TIDE cliffs

36 Point

QUILT corner highly

COOPER BLACK ITALIC

48 Point

MUSICIAN instruments

36 Point

SYMPHONIES? Rhythm & Time

14 Point

THE CHARMING Music of this piece is woven round the very beautiful theme which at the

30 Point

SOUND! Recitals

12 Point

IT WILL, NO DOUBT, be appreciated that, as in the Orchestral Score, which, considering the many and varied ways and also the very

24 Point

DANCING 2nd & 3rd items will

10 Point

THE TRUE TRIUMPH OF Musical Genius consists in having created a work which produces by its very perfection an effect on the musical mind which, being in harmony with all the other lighter and graceful

18 Point

MOVEMENTS 'Appassionata' Played at all the principal

BODONI LIGHT

14 Point

THOSE VISITORS WHO ride or walk through its busy streets will recall with interest the fact that this part dominates the whole Metropolis. During the last

12 Point

NO TRAVELLER WILL BE unduly surprised or amazed at the magnitude of things that he sees, for the fact that this or that is the largest of its kind in the world is rarely left unemphasized. But though it

10 Point

ROADS LEAD THROUGH TALL forests, interrupted at intervals by lakes and streams and waterfalls. Varied and arresting beauty, and facilities for every outdoor sport confront the visitor everywhere. They are enjoyed the more on account of the large and spacious

8 Point

SHARP CONTRASTS CAN BE NOTED in the character of its main streets and chief buildings, some of which time has not modernised. An outstanding place of interest is the lovely mountain park which all travellers should make a point of visiting. From all parts of the world people come to see this magnificent and spectacular phenomenon, considered by

6 Point

THAT THIS IS ONE OF THE WONDERS OF the world, none could doubt. Standing at one of the many points of vantage, a feeling of awe, and a sensation of indescribable majesty and power, comes even to the most widely travelled visitor. A world famous traveller, standing on a promontory overlooking this wonder of nature, exclaimed : "If people only knew or could see the splendid things here, of the exhilaration and fascination of these outdoor enjoyments offered through a vacation spent

36 Point

COLOURS bring us joy and often it

30 Point

QUADRANT fourth part of a circle. This section nearly

24 Point

RISING FROM out of the sea like a mirage, its splendid and far-reaching natural

18 Point

BROADWAY CUTS an irregular course of many miles through Manhattan. It is first a business street, very broad and busy, and

BODONI MEDIUM

36 Point

YOU CAN
if you will

30 Point

THIS TOUR
may be made
in a reverse

24 Point

THE RETURN
journey brings
passengers back
to the hotel for

18 Point

A VISIT IS NOT
complete without a
trip on this famous
lake, the longest and
considered the most

14 Point

CONSPICUOUS FOR ITS
high bridge and gigantic
power station marks the
first steep ascent. From
this point each view seems
to surpass in beauty its

72 Point

LIVE
jolly?

60 Point

SEND
bigger!

48 Point

QUEEN
queenly

42 Point

AT ONE
of the 1st

23

BODONI BOLD

36 Point

SINGING
dancing &

30 Point

THEATRE
opera house

24 Point

CONDUCTOR
the auditorium

18 Point

**THE FAUTEUILS
are considered the**

14 Point

**THIS MODERN AND
brilliant musical fantasy**

12 Point

**THE PROGRAMME HAS
a special appeal to all who**

10 Point

**THIS PIECE, WHICH WAS
designed to connect the 1st
movement of the theme with**

8 Point

**CROWNED BY THE PLAUDITS
of the world as monarch of living
pianists, no other who ever lived has
had such a wonderful career as**

6 Point

**THE MUSIC FORESHADOWS THE OPENING
scene of the act, the composer having very
cleverly translated the atmosphere of the scene
into music. This composition, although one
of his earliest attempts, was considered to be**

72 Point

LIFE
jolly!

60 Point

JUNE
gaily?

48 Point

PIANO
greatly

42 Point

ORGAN
blowers

ULTRA BODONI

60 Point

IN SOME types for

48 Point

IT WAS IN 1927 that a

42 Point

THE LATEST facilities give

36 Point

WHEN a great

24 Point

DISTINCT because of its superb

30 Point

QUITE A new and

18 Point

IN PLEASING and effective contrast, this

NUBIAN

60 Point

MOST rotary

48 Point

PARTS of 125 &

42 Point

QUITE A good rate

36 Point

FOR some

24 Point

OFTEN the few reverse

30 Point

CARE on the

18 Point

DEVICES for many occasions

NEULAND

30 Point

ADVERTISING IS INFLUENCED BY

24 Point

IN 1924, WHEN THE PRODUCTION OF AN

18 Point (No. 1)

IDEAS THAT WERE VERY EFFECTIVE MANY YEARS AGO AND DESIGNS WHICH

18 Point (No. 2)

EVERYBODY WAS FAMILIAR WITH THE WONDERFUL AND COMMENDABLE QUALITY OF

14 Point

IN EARLY ADVERTISING DAYS, ART HAD NOT BEEN THOUGHT OF IN CONNECTION WITH POSTER PUBLICITY. AS MUCH AS £8,350

12 Point

THE LEADING AND MOST DECISIVE FACTORS CLAIMED BY THE MAJORITY

10 Point

IT CANNOT BE TOO STRONGLY URGED AT THE OUTSET THAT IN NEARLY EVERY CASE WHERE EFFICIENCY HAS

27

NARCISS

30 Point

HERE IS
the latest

24 Point

AS FAR AS
knowledge &

18 Point

IN COUNTRY,
Town and City

14 Point

IT WAS IN THE
year 1896, that a
certain section of

12 Point

ON ACCOUNT OF
the immense altitude,
estimated at more than
23,571 feet above sea

10 Point

MINERAL RESOURCES
of parts of the country
are found to be very
valuable, and it has been
thought by the so-called

8 Point

THE STATES AND ALSO A
considerable number of the
provinces are to many very
interesting, as, on those rare
occasions, which the majority
of travellers fortunate enough

72 Point

JET
blue

60 Point

SUN
light

48 Point

STAR
shines

36 Point

WHY?
because

MAX AND FOURNIER-LE-JEUNE

36 Point MAX

SALES
MUST

28 Point

TRADES
FOLDER

20 Point

FACTORY
METHODS
1827 · 1927

16 Point

EDUCATION
MODERNISES
AS FAR AS IS
POSSIBLE TO

14 Point

COLOURS USED
SPARINGLY SO
AS TO ENABLE
DECORATIONS

12 Point

COLOURS THAT
PLEASE THE EYE
NATURE'S OWN
ADVERTISEMENT
MOST BEAUTIFUL
COLOUR EFFECTS

24 Point FOURNIER-LE-JEUNE

*INSURE
SAFETY
POLICY*

20 Point

*YOU CAN
TAKE THE
FIRST OF
THE BEST*

18 Point

*DECORATED
CATALOGUE
COLOURS OF
THE BEST &*

29

CHARCOAL and BULLETIN

48 Point Charcoal

It is impossible to
describe these 1st

36 Point

The Charming Colours
and the Delicacy of this
Graceful Masterpiece

24 Point

There are many Beautiful Specimens
of colouring to be seen and admired,
and of the 27 Exhibits, particular
attention is very often drawn to those

36 Point Bulletin

Hanging in very Graceful
Folds, this exquisite and

24 Point

Here again one is held spellbound by
the extreme delicacy of the formations,
and by the wealth of colouring which

SAMSON

84 Point

A Yearly

72 Point

Over 72,834

54 Point

This distinction was considered

42 Point

Every possible point consistent with these

36 Point

Classification took nearly 10 years before eventually

30 Point

Nothing can be said in favour of the many and varied ways

SCOTCH ROMAN

30 Point

MAKE IT
concise and

24 Point

GET INTO
touch with a

18 Point

THEY CAN BE
arranged to suit
every pocket and

14 Point

THE OBJECT OF
this is to find the total
number of chargeable
hours for the year so

12 Point

A TRUE SERVICE IS
rendered the public when
good goods are sold to the
public and distributed by
satisfied dealers. The cost

10 Point

THE POSTER IS ONE OF THE
oldest of advertising mediums but
has been the very latest to develop
artistically. It was not until the
period of the world war for liberty
loan and red cross appeals that our

8 Point

THE BEST OF THE ORIGINAL
fancy borderings have survived to the
present day and, in addition, we have
an unlimited array of modern ornament
from which to draw. Type can now be
interspersed with em-sized flowers, and
these smallest of units often combine in

72 Point

WE
gold

60 Point

TOP
high

48 Point

STEM
for the

36 Point

REFER
you to 24

32

SCOTCH ROMAN ITALIC and PLYMOUTH ITALIC

30 Point Scotch Roman Italic

OBJECT objection &

24 Point

IT IS AT least 4 or 5

18 Point

A DISTINCT number of styles

14 Point

THE CHARMING features and present taste for colours in

12 Point

THE IMPRESSION made by authentic Italian Renaissance furniture is one of grandeur. While

10 Point

ONE DECIDED ADVANCE marked the opening of this period and accounts for some of its outstanding features. Modern forms of this style provide the charm of the

8 Point

THE STYLE VERY GRADUALLY became ornate, and flutings, groovings, beardings and other ornamentation were lavishly used. The most familiar detail is the scroll, which appears in a wide range, from plain to the present fancy

6 Point

ALTHOUGH THEY WERE ARCHITECTS the two brothers instituted a distinctive style of furniture primarily to match the houses they designed. In contrast with the furniture of their contemporaries, their style featured decoration rather than form, adopting the straight forms typical of the designers of

36 Point Plymouth Italic

BOTH 1 and 3

30 Point

QUEEN queenly!

24 Point

DESIGN & styles

18 Point

THE SAME magnificent

12 Point

CHARACTERISED by splendour, ease and luxury, it was

10 Point

THIS ARM CHAIR made its appearance towards the end of the reign of Louis X, and

8 Point

LOUIS X FURNITURE represents the essence of refinement: sensible, graceful proportions are outstanding qualities. The style shows a

6 Point

SOME AUTHORITIES SAY that the return to the classic preceded the reign of Louis, whereas others credit the simple-mannered Queen with influencing the trend to the classic. There is this distinction

33

BODONI MEDIUM ITALIC and OLD FACE ITALIC

18 Point Bodoni Medium Italic

FACTS, REASONS and Ideas dominate every Business, and although essentially

36 Point Old Face Italic

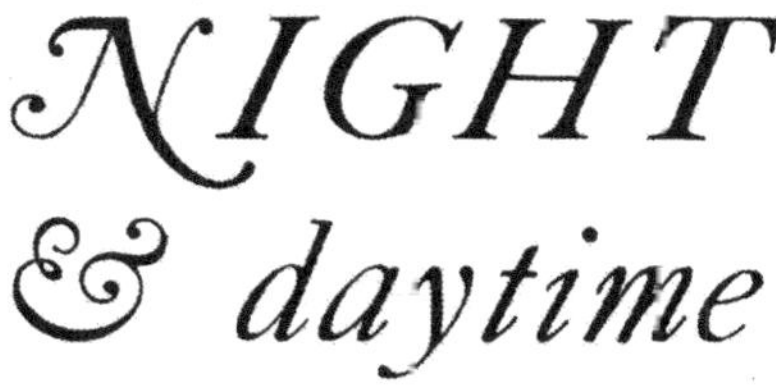

14 Point

NO MATTER WHAT Poor Printing costs, it is not worth what you pay for it. Printing has the same relation to business

30 Point

ECONOMY often produces

12 Point

THE EXTRA COST OF quality in Printing is Insurance against poor returns. Printing is the seed sown by the successful enterprises, small and great. Poor seeds, small crops. Poor printing

24 Point

PROGRESS IS essential when the

18 Point

POOR PRINTING gives the impression to

10 Point

NONE BUT A FOOLISH MAN would expect good crops from poor seeds, and poor crops are by far the more expensive crops. They cost just as much as good crops for plowing, harrowing and cultivating. Yet there are farmers who prefer to save a few foolish pounds for seed outlay rather than expend them

14 Point

THE EXTRA COST when considered against

12 Point

REMEMBER! SUCCESS in any line depends upon the use of constructive arguments to

10 Point

NO BUSINESS IS SO SMALL that it may not be benefited to a certain extent by the aid of Printing. The policy that prompts the business man and

8 Point

PUT QUALITY INTO ALL YOUR advertising—selling quality—and you will find it a force, not a luxury—a motive power in busines, not a drag on the wheels. Successful advertising carries the suggestion of quality—quality that comes from thought in every line. The success of advertising depends on what is said in the message; how it is duplicated; how it is carried to those who read it and what readers it is carried to. These things influence to a

8 Point

THE LARGER A BUSINESS, THE more vital Printing is to its progress. None but a foolish man will expect good returns from poor printing. Yet there are many shrewd business men of to-day who, if they were to

OLD FACE

14 Point

THE OLD MASTERS of printing, and printers who have achieved fame, have kept in view several qualities. In the first instance their books are characterised by the great simplicity of style. The

12 Point

THE CHOICE OF TYPE depends partly on the paper to be used. A rough paper needs a thicker type than a smooth one. Ugly type can ruin a book otherwise good, and therefore it is well to have beautiful type. It is not only the type itself that matters but also the way of

10 Point

The successful designer must keep himself conversant with the best current work of the day. He should notice carefully the founts and the materials used by good printers and their special methods of gaining their effects. Happily such examples are within the reach of all. If the job is intended to be worked in one colour only endeavour to obtain the necessary light and shade by the judicious distribution of strong faced

8 Point

A good designer is a man of ready resource, capable of making the most of the material with which he has to work, and ever quick to catch an idea, or to develop a new combination from old materials. It is futile for the designer to say that if he only had certain kinds of type or ornament he could turn out something artistic, and that it is no use trying with the poor stuff at his command. He must use what he possesses to the very best advantage. It is often surprising to find how many variations can be made from a limited quantity of material. A border may be often

36 Point

SALE OF goods and therefore a

30 Point

SOME MEN can pay very little for their printing; yet

24 Point

A SPECIMEN shown in No. 27 supplement was taken from one of the beautiful

18 Point

THE AGE OF THE haphazard advertisement has gone, too. To-day you will find that in nearly every advertisement that it

35

18 Point

DISTINCTION and originality are the secrets of success in the present system

14 Point

FACTS, REASONS and ideas dominate in business, and must necessarily be used to bring about desire by prospective buyer

12 Point

THE HUMOUR OF A phrase does not add to its ultimate effectiveness; apparently it does assure quicker response however. Humour usually creates confidence which decides

10 Point

THE FIRST NECESSITY of criticism is that of a standard. Without a definite standard there can be no measurement of work. There is no estimating the truth or falsity of anything unless there is first some idea of truth; the merit and the worthlessness

8 Point

THE USE OF SENSATIONAL phrases is not relished particularly by some newspapers readers. Such phrases certainly contain a great human-interest appeal for most of those who peruse them. A newspaper to hold the attention of its readers must use powerful headlines containing just sufficient information to create curiosity to follow it up. Keen salesmen must always gain the

42 Point

TRIM lengths

36 Point

VIEWS scenery April, 27

30 Point

COLOUR decorated beautifully & adorned

24 Point

QUESTION The Answer is descriptive interesting & of real value

GARAMOND and BOOKLET

18 Point Garamond

IF YOU COULD look over the man's shoulder when he receives your book it may surprise you

14 Point

A GOOD PICTURE IS not a good poster-design. A picture of merit is only appreciated fully on close inspection such as is not accorded to a poster, and

12 Point

TO-DAY THE AVERAGE advertiser is not fully aware of the possibilities before him in compelling reproduction. It is a common thought that illustrations in line are simply cheap and least effective from

10 Point

YOU WANT A PRINTER WHO understands ; one who can adhere to the details of your layout, and use common sense in the things left to his discretion ; one who can visualize the job as you visualize it yourself, and create reality out of the dream ; one who can point to

8 Point

THE FACT THAT NO MAN WITH taste would hang a poster that knows its job on the walls of his dining-room may be the highest praise, even when that poster is in all other respects a pleasant work of art. The appeal, the range, the intention, are all so vitally different. We hear, and read, a great deal about the modern designs and the unique wonders

36 Point

PRINT & the best of

30 Point

THE LAST started within the actual 48

24 Point

THERE WAS another secret behind the big

12 Point Booklet

IT IS NOT OUT OF place here to put in a word with regard to the unique methods usually employed by a

10 Point

TRUE EFFICIENCY IN business, even more than consistency, is a jewel — a thing of special value, of rare excellence. In the interest of true efficiency, most men aim

8 Point

TIME AND EDUCATION WILL take care of such conditions, and eventually we shall learn to face the facts. Meanwhile, we make our bow and our exit, gracefully we trust, but with a sure sense of conscious rectitude, hoping that in

37

GARAMOND ITALIC and CLOISTER BOLD ITALIC

18 Point

THIS MODEL IS constructed on exactly the same lines as the luxurious and beautiful

14 Point

WITH A LIGHT PULL on the strap beneath the overlay, the seat rises with well balanced movement and comes forward. Enclosed in such

12 Point

TO HAVE IN THE home a settee which, in addition to its usefulness as a handsome piece of furniture can be used in an emergency or occasionally as a bed, is indeed an economy of

10 Point

THIS OAK CANE SETTEE has an air of solidity, and its high back makes it as comfortable as it is decorative. It has proved to be a very popular model, and gives no outward appearance of its dual purpose. The extreme length and also the depth are

8 Point

THE MODEL ILLUSTRATED IS very suitable where space must be economised or where a smaller settee is preferred, the overall length being 3 ft. 6 in. It is also made in separate sections which can be taken apart and re-assembled quite easily. This model is upholstered with the finest quality fibre and wool on steel springs, and is also

36 Point Garamond Italic

MODELS 1 & 3 are

30 Point

THERE IS a design to suit

24 Point

IT CAN BE taken to pieces if the occasion should

36 Point Cloister Bold Italic

A VERY attractive &

24 Point

ESTABLISHED since 1860, and

18 Point

PROBABLY IT IS not thought possible to improve on such a

38

20 Point

HONORABLE
distinguished manner
which attracts great

18 Point

THE ADVENT OF
the paper manufacturer
into advertising is most
certainly taking a very

16 Point

KNOWLEDGE AND
success in life is the amount
of knowledge gained which
can be used in an effective
manner so as to promote quite

14 Point

ART LOVERS IN THIS
country are familiar with the
colour prints made at The Forest
Press of Hesketh Hubbard, the
artist, which is in Breamore, near
Salisbury, England and they will

12 Point

PRINTING TO-DAY IS IN
the same condition as the periodicals
of to-day—under their hand is a
potential field of such infinitely vast
proportions that present business,
large as it is, would look diminutive
as compared to it. This business will
continue to remain the same until it
is visualised by those responsible for

72 Point

NIL
deliver

48 Point

MAN
fountains

36 Point

SKETCH
effective pens
always retain

30 Point

ESSENCES
delightful spring
fragrance and the
most beautiful of

39

NICOLAS COCHIN ITALIC

18 Point

AS WITH THE man, so with the work of his hands and brain. His products (whether merchandise or thought) can always be relied upon

16 Point

TRUE EFFICIENCY in business, even more than consistency, is a jewel—a thing of very special value, of rare excellence. In the interest of true efficiency, most men aim to get the very best

14 Point

ALL ADVERTISING IS based on something written—then circulated. This circulation may be by Newspaper or Periodical, or by Letter, Booklet or other mediums. It is very important to remember that advertising should always be logical and reasonable.

12 Point

THE FIRST NECESSITY OF Criticism is that of a standard. There is no estimating the truth or falsity of anything unless there is first some idea of truth ; the merit and the worthlessness of a thing cannot be m e a s u r e d unless there be some ideal by which it may be judged. Whatever view the critic takes it is very essential that those concerned

48 Point

POST excellent

6 Point

POSTER consideration must demand

30 Point

BUSINESS! What in 1923 was thought to perhaps be one of

20 Point

THE RESULTS of this labour and co-operation began to be very apparent in the early stages of

40

NICOLAS COCHIN BOLD

20 Point

FROM ALL
parts of the world
people travel to

72 Point

FIX
black

18 Point

VISITORS ARE
invariably impressed
by the exquisite and
most beautiful colours

48 Point

DAYS
months

16 Point

STANDING ON A
promontory overlooking
the landscape, far away
in the distance can just be
seen what is perhaps the

14 Point

HERE IS VARIED
and natural beauty, glorious
scenery and also interesting
cities — a place for novel,
engrossing pleasure travel.
For those who are fond of

36 Point

ROUTE
interesting
because we

12 Point

THE MOST ELOQUENT
description of the alluring and
scenic beauty of the surrounding
country must be inadequate.
The environs are of endless
charm, and among the many
delightful and picturesque parts
there are to be seen gives some

30 Point

STEAMER
1st & 3rd class
to Amsterdam

41

PLANTIN

24 Point

TO THOSE
who achieve

18 Point

NATURALLY
the opportunities

14 Point

SUCH IS A RAPID
review of progress
during the time since

12 Point

THERE IS AT LEAST
no limit to the definite
improvements of which
even yet it is capable, so

10 Point

THE PRODUCTS OF THE
present will inevitably be in
the future eclipsed, just as the
achievements of the past have
been outshone by those of

8 Point

FROM THIS WE LEARN THAT
results are gained by setting forth
the constructive facts, and not by
the other methods usually employed.
Many in the past did not realise this,
and even up to the present time such

6 Point

THE FIRST NECESSITY IS THAT OF A
standard. Without definite standards there can
be no real measurement of work. There is no
estimating the truth or falsity of anything unless there is first some idea of truth, and the
merit or worthlessness of a thing cannot be
measured unless there be some idea by which
it may be judged. Although it may appear to

60 Point

ASK
now!

48 Point

TIME
years?

42 Point

DAYS
months

36 Point

WEEK
hours &

30 Point

TO-DAY
60 minutes

PLANTIN ITALIC

18 Point

AGAIN ONE IS held spell-bound by the delicacy of the formation and

14 Point

THE WONDERFUL model has been very aptly described, and rightly so, as " The finest Stalactite in the

12 Point

THE MULTITUDE OF stalactites suspended from the roof is seen reflected in pools of crystal-clear water, until it appears that one is looking upon a miniature

10 Point

SEVERAL INSTANCES still obtain of Stalactites and Stalagmites having become one, a joining-up process that has in many cases taken thousands of years. It is interesting to note that since the discovery of these

8 Point

THERE ARE MANY SPLENDID specimens of colouring to be seen on the walls and here one's attention is drawn in particular to the clefts in the rock walls, and to the vaulted roof. Here, too, is to be seen what is perhaps the finest view of the various other formations, which, considering the extreme difficulties to be

48 Point

BEST beauty

36 Point

JEWEL palaces &

30 Point

TRAVEL by road or other routes

24 Point

PRIVATE! enclosed with over 150 other fine & unique

43

VESTA

30 Point

TO UNDERSTAND AND APPRECIATE THESE QUALITIES

24 Point

PERFECTION HAS ONLY BEEN ACQUIRED SINCE THE INNOVATION OF

18 Point

IN 1927, A HIGHER DEGREE OF EFFICIENCY WAS OBTAINED. CHARACTERISTIC IN ALL THE ATTRACTIVE DETAILS WHICH

14 Point

THE FRUITION OF THIS WONDERFUL ACHIEVEMENT AND THE PROGRESSIVE POLICY PURSUED DURING THE MANY ARDUOUS AND SEEMINGLY IMPOSSIBLE

12 Point

A DEPARTMENT OF EXPERIMENT AND RESEARCH BECAME NECESSARY, AND IN ORGANIZING SUCH A

10 Point

THE IMPROVEMENTS AND IDEALS WHICH WERE TO BE ACCOMPLISHED WERE NOT QUESTIONS OF USING BETTER MATERIAL OR THE COLLABORATION OF SUCH

30 Point Hallamshire

DISTANCE
between the
2nd and 4th

48 Point

HELP
helpful

24 Point

EXPOSURES
in photography
are more often
governed by an

36 Point

HOME &
friends are

18 Point

IT IS WELL TO
recognise that just
as good technique is
essential to the best
results, so is correct

12 Point Kennerley

IN FACT, THE ARTIST
should be predominant be-
fore the exposure is made,
and later when the printing
medium, the colour and the

14 Point

IN PICTURE-TAKING
we are concerned mostly
with exposure, develop-
ment, printing, toning and
such chemical processes as
are necessary to obtain a

10 Point

AERIAL PHOTOGRAPHY.
These notes have been compiled
from actual experience in the
air. It was by adopting such
methods as broadly indicated
here that the majority of these

12 Point

ART IN PHOTOGRAPHY
is most concerned with correct
selection and composition of a
subject, its taking under the best
conditions of atmosphere and
lighting, and its presentation as
a print. Satisfactory results as

8 Point

THE FACTORS GIVEN MAY BE
altered to suit individual requirements.
It is only necessary to remember that
decreasing the factor lessens contrast.
Exposure controls the density of the
negative; alteration in the factor controls the contrast. Judge the results by

6 Point

A FEW GENERAL HINTS. WHERE IT IS
possible, always operate through base of fusilage.
When making an exposure do not contract the
muscles of the fingers quickly, or the result will
show general movement. The action should be
as the release of a rifle trigger, or a very gentle
squeeze. See that the lens is set before ascending
and make sure it will remain so. On no account

45

CHELTENHAM WIDE AND GLOUCESTER

18 Point

IF IT IS YOUR
desire to purchase
a piano which will

14 Point

THE INSTRUMENTS
shown are but few of the
many models of these
famous pianos.   All are

12 Point

IT IS NOT EVERYONE
who realizes the advantage
that infallibly result from
dealing with a great selling
organisation, but a minute

10 Point

THROUGH THE MEDIUM OF
the new self-governed pneumatic
action, especially prepared music
rolls, the actual performances of
leading pianists are reproduced
with all the charm, spirit and tone

8 Point

THOSE EMINENT MUSICIANS WHO
have heard this piano and have recorded
their performances for it, are unmeasured
in their enthusiastic praises of extra-
ordinary powers of faithful reproduction.
The electric models are driven exclusively
by electric power, foot-operated models

6 Point

YOU AND YOUR FRIENDS CAN HEAR THE
world's finest music, dance or jazz and the latest
songs. For years it has been acclaimed the finest
and most beautiful of all instruments. Every one
that leaves the factory is of the best construction.
The constant striving to surpass the previous best,
and the producing of enormous variety of instruments, this is helpful and well worth remembering

72 Point Cheltenham Wide

HIM

story

42 Point

THESE
were the

36 Point

ON THE
west of us
are the 17

24 Point Gloucester

SEND NOW
for some of our
most famous

46

GLOUCESTER BOLD and CHELTENHAM BOLD

36 Point Gloucester Bold

TEACH
technical

30 Point

APPEARS
disappears

24 Point

SERVICES &
the potential

18 Point

ATTENTION IS
often directed to

14 Point

AUTHORISED AND
regarded by qualified

12 Point

**DEVELOPMENTS THAT
have been formulated for**

10 Point

**READILY APPRECIATED WAS
the economical publicity which
not only was found beneficial in**

8 Point

**EDUCATION & TIME EVENTUALLY
will take care of such influential and
effective policies. Meanwhile, hoping
that the many deductions and natural**

6 Point

**THIS SUCCESS WILL BE FOUND MAINLY
to depend upon (1) What is said in the message ;
(2) How it is duplicated ; (3) How it is carried
to those who read it ; (4) What readers it is
carried to. These things, chiefly, to a great**

72 Point Cheltenham Bold

PET
soft!

60 Point

FIVE
eight

48 Point

USED
by the

42 Point

STAFF
and 1st

47

CHELTENHAM BOLD ITALIC, CHELTENHAM ITALIC and
GLOUCESTER ITALIC

36 Point Cheltenham Bold Italic

*MODEL
interests*

30 Point

*CLASSIC
a classical*

24 Point

*QUALITIES
the quality of*

18 Point

*ADVANTAGES
these advantages*

14 Point

*A TREMENDOUS
flexibility, with that*

12 Point

*IT IS NOT EVERYONE
who realizes the benefits*

10 Point

*TESTIMONY AS TO THE
outstanding merits which
have been enumerated, has*

8 Point

*THE DELICACY & PRECISION
of tone and action are considered
by competent experts and judges to
be unsurpassed, and the exceptional*

30 Point Cheltenham Italic

*SMALLER
but equal to a*

24 Point

*OF BRITISH
design & offered*

18 Point

*ADVANTAGES
obtain amongst the*

14 Point

*SERIES OF WELL
chosen and interesting*

12 Point Gloucester Italic

*IN AN ILLUMINATING
paragraph two or three of the
main " influences" to be noted*

10 Point

*THESE OPENING SKETCHES
communicate by their implications the
calming influences that are such a
pleasing contrast to previous examples.*

8 Point

*THESE ILLUSTRATIONS CLEARLY
show the possibilities of the method, and it
is thought quite feasible, and at the same time
perfectly intelligible to the complete novice if
the interpretations, as clearly treated earlier*

6 Point

*THAT THE PLAN IS NOVEL THERE CAN
be no question, and that it is a sound and practical
one is attested by the approval and active co-operation
of the finest minds engaged in this profession. It must
occur to everyone that the width of this approval is
unique. Assuredly, never before in the history of this*

48

CHELTENHAM BOLD CONDENSED

36 Point

JOURNALS
journalistic

30 Point

MAGAZINES
and periodicals

24 Point

NEWSPAPERS &
books for every

18 Point

AN ESSENTIAL AND
instructive manual to

14 Point

THE FIRST PUBLICATION
will be welcomed by those

12 Point

ITS BRIGHTLY-WRITTEN AND
breezy contents, which include

10 Point

THE MANY CHAPTER HEADINGS,
which will be noticed is an entirely
new feature, help to give a better

8 Point

VERY NEATLY PRINTED IN TWO COLOURS
on very fine art paper, with a pleasing and
attractive cover and handsomely bound, this
publication will afford much pleasure to those

6 Point

HERE IS A BOOK YOU WILL WANT TO READ
and keep handy by you ever afterwards for future
reference. It crystallises in a most readable manner
the long experience and truly happy inspirations of
a leading authority on this subject. There are many

72 Point

REST
might

60 Point

TRIAL
verdict

48 Point

RESULT
of the 67

42 Point

QUERY?
questions

49

CHELTENHAM BOLD EXPANDED

36 Point

PRINT
printer

30 Point

GUARD
protects

24 Point

TRAINER
and rider

18 Point

INFORMERS
information

14 Point

DESCRIPTIONS
and illustrations

12 Point

RECONNAISSANCE
is to survey with a

10 Point

A CONTEMPORARY
painting & engraving

8 Point

IT IS UPON THE BASIS OF
a psychological experience
that rests the method and

6 Point

SUCH A COMBINATION IS ONLY
achieved by the application of
the resources of modern science
applied by the skill of a greater

72 Point

GO
the

60 Point

INK
pen

48 Point

WET
drier

42 Point

BLUE
black

72 Point

PRINT MIX

coupon type

60 Point

PAPERS SELL

sent for roads

48 Point

CLASS OF FINAL

letter that sale of

36 Point

READ WHAT SORTER

some business for works

men and others

24 Point

THE GREAT

say about the sales that are

CHELTENHAM BOLD SHADED

30 Point

IN ORDER
to ensure a
restful and
correct way

60 Point

GIRL
fresh!

24 Point

VARIATION
of tone and
action depend
upon 12 very
simple & easy

48 Point

MOST
of this

18 Point

GRADUATION
in proportion to
accompaniment is
effected by using,
or, as sometimes
is preferred by a

42 Point

FOR A
detailed

14 Point

ALL CHANGES, AS
well as all the other
expression indications
should be put into
immediate effect the
moment such changes
or indications appear

36 Point

TO-DAY
the many
details of

52

JOHN HANCOCK

36 Point

BREEZE & gentle

30 Point

ESSENCE perfumes

24 Point

PRODUCING one million

18 Point

BEAUTIFULLY decorated with

14 Point

FINAL EDITION OF newspapers with

12 Point

THE WISEST MINDS are the most teachable

10 Point

COST MAY BE DEFINED as the sum total of all the expenses incurred

8 Point

THE DIFFERENCE BETWEEN printing with type and the art of printing with type can be emphasized and the idea

6 Point

THE PRIMARY INTERPRETATION of calligraphy is 'fine' writing. This interpretation is given preference because the early calligraphers had such respect for their craft that only

72 Point

SET pail

60 Point

RIM trail

48 Point

SLOT coins

42 Point

MORE than 12

53

JOHN HANCOCK CONDENSED

36 Point
BEAUTIFUL
colour and

30 Point
IT IS A LIGHT
oil which does

24 Point
ONLY BY USING
this can you be

18 Point
**EACH MAN IS GIVEN
a day and his work
for the day, and once,**

14 Point
**THERE IS WAITING THE
work where only hands
can avail, and so, if he
falters, a chord in music**

12 Point
**YES, THE TASK THAT IS GIVEN
to each man no other can do,
so the errand is waiting—it
has waited through ages for
you, and now you appear;**

72 Point
PENS
write

60 Point
TRAIL
query

48 Point
MONEY
pound £

42 Point
ANSWER
questions

54

ROYCROFT OPEN and ROYCROFT

60 Point Roycroft Open

SUIT
1 & 2

60 Point Roycroft

SUIT
1 & 2

48 Point

HOME
garden

48 Point

HOME
garden

36 Point

STAIRS
escalator

36 Point

STAIRS
escalator

24 Point

COMFORTS
comfortable

24 Point

COMFORTS
comfortable

18 Point

ATTRACTIVE
and effective on

18 Point

ATTRACTIVE
and effective on

10 Point Roycroft

THIS DESIGN, WHICH
has a nicely carved frame
of Jacobean oak, would be
a decorative addition for

12 Point

THIS UNIQUE AND
luxurious design is often
regarded by the eminent

55

ADTYPE

30 Point

LET THEM go now for the book of

24 Point

ANY MAN IS wealthy who has a happy home and a

18 Point

WHEN GIVEN A little thought, it is not regarded otherwise than a good idea for an

12 Point

MANY OTHER VISIONS rise before us, and ruling all is the strange belief in man as a strong creature, naturally thought of as being of muscular build

10 Point

COME TO THE QUESTION "What is success?" Is it the attainment of a set ideal? Are we, when that ideal is reached, to sit back and say I am content? Nothing could make me more contented. I

60 Point

SOFT fur &

48 Point

APRIL has 30

42 Point

MEDAL won by the best

36 Point

STRONG mind and good will

56

WESTMINSTER and COCHIN OPEN

18 Point Westminster

IT IS, PERHAPS, not without significance that there are manufacturers who sometimes in

14 Point

AT THE OUTSET it is very difficult to be dogmatic, which is, perhaps, as well, although when it is remembered that in 1923 a complete

12 Point

IN REGARD TO GOODS, either for the home or elsewhere, which are purchased out of capital, and are to be used over a lengthy period, the British origin must not be disregarded, as is very

10 Point

I DO NOT WANT TO GO into technical details except of the most general kind, because their description would only tend to confuse the mind. But in speaking of the processes other than the simplest, it is not generally appreciated that a

8 Point

PURPLE AND BLUE ARE MUCH affected by this firm in the tints for its illustrations, with a relieving black as a third colour. Red and yellow is another effective combination for this purpose, but it is a practice, though not, perhaps, a rule in these matters, that the tints shall be pale. The uncommonness of the whole design must be continued in the colours,

30 Point Cochin Open

OUT OF THE 6 & 7 LONG

24 Point

MUCH OF the work of today has been built upon the scientific and

18 Point

A TRADITION, with its roots buried in the past has been created, which has, so to speak, mellowed the harshness of work and invested it with

14 Point

THE POLICY? IT IS this! Let us view it with the correct mental attitude. The policy that prompts the manufacturer to advertise to a buyer is basically sound. It also produces a very great element as regards the medium that has

57

WREN AND COMSTOCK

48 Point Wren

BLUE
and red

48 Point Comstock—Full Face

MAKE

36 Point—Full Face

ROMAN

30 Point

COLOURS
1, 2 & 3 fine

36 Point

CRITIC
modify

24 Point

VERY LIGHT
effects are often
obtainable during

30 Point

SKETCH
effective

18 Point

THE NATURAL
colouring and also the
pleasing brown and
grey designs over the

24 Point

PROBLEM
difficulties

18 Point

QUESTIONS?
Nos. 12 & 34

12 Point

THESE PURE WHITE
deposits, formed by the
percolation of water through
lime-charged strata from the
hills, mingle with those of

14 Point

**PLEASE NOTICE!
Here are facilities
to those who wish**

58

TYPEWRITER

Mono No. 2. 12 Point

We beg to inform you that the 1927
Edition of the above Journal - REVISED AND
CORRECTED TO DATE - will be published early
in April. It will contain a complete list

Remington No. 2. 12 Point

It reaches EVERY SEAPORT and practically
everyone of importance connected with the
Foreign ADMIRALTIES and NAVIES, in addition
to Shipowners. A limited number are sent to

Yost. 12 Point

The advertisement rate for a WHOLE page
for ONE YEAR is £10/10/0, HALF page £6/0/0,
QUARTER page £3/5/0. A copy of the Book
will be given free of charge to every one

Oliver Printype. 12 Point

This Publication is the ONLY ONE OF
ITS KIND. It has a weekly circulation of
10,000 copies; is sold all over the world.
Every ship has at least one copy on board

Yankee Remington. 12 Point

This is a very important point for
advertisers, who are thus assured of a
GREAT CIRCULATION in towns not usually
reached by Shipping Journals. You will get

New Style Remington. 12 Point

This class of journal has been proved
a most PROFITABLE INVESTMENT to a large
number of Advertisers. It is the only paper
read by the majority of prospective clients

Old Typewriter. 12 Point

With reference to the enclosed, we
suggest that OUR series of journals are best
for your notices. Printed on ART PAPER and
in clear type, the cost is 1/- per MONTH or

59

TYPEWRITER

Oliver No. 3. 12 Point

We enclose a SPECIMEN QUOTATION for
your consideration and should you decide to
take advantage of this excellent scheme
send at once to us for our new booklet, it

Oliver No. 4. 12 Point

I should be very pleased to send you a
form, with FULL PARTICULARS, on hearing
from you as to your requirements. Orders
from 20/- carriage paid any distance. We

Smith Premier. 12 Point

The enclosed Circular deals with our
SALE, and we feel sure it will be well
worth your while to visit us on JULY 1st.
We are confident it will be to our mutual

New Model Smith Premier. 12 Point

We may say further, that in addition to
the models mentioned, we have a LIMITED
NUMBER of instruments at prices from £65 to
£100. Every one is guaranteed to last four

Elite. 10 Point

This Special Offer has been arranged for
the benefit of past purchasers of our stock. Turn
to the enclosed catalogue and see what you save by
sending in your order now. In addition to these

Yost. 10 Point

We have great pleasure in enclosing our new
PRICE LIST. Both TRADE and RETAIL prices will come
into force on February 20th, and will remain so
until further notice from us. You will notice it

6 Point

Comparatively few exporters in this country know of the vast area of
the Country mentioned, with its population of over sixty millions. With its
Oil Wells, Gold, Tin and Coal Mines, its innumerable Tea, Coffee, Rubber and
Sugar Estates, and 200 Docks and Harbours, it affords a market unexcelled in
the Far East. The experienced administration of the Government ensures
stability, WHILST THERE ARE NO CURRENCY PROBLEMS, theirs being practically

60

SPARTAN BOLD and COPPERPLATE

18 Point Spartan Bold

I WILL REMEMBER MY

18 Point Small Caps

HE ORDERED ME A SEVENTY

12 Point

IN A LARGER WAY, I HAVE 149

12 Point Small Caps

I MAILED THREE THOUSAND LETTERS,

10 Point

AND THIS IS THE REASON WHY NO ADVER-

10 Point Small Caps

CURIOSITY IS A TWO-EDGED SWORD; LIKE ALL

6 Point

ART LOVERS IN THIS COUNTRY ARE FAMILIAR WITH COLOUR

5 Point on 6

THIS HONEST, DEPENDABLE, HARD-HEADED GROUP OF MEN IS NOT EASILY

4 Point on 6

THIS SHOWED ME THAT HALF OF THE YEARLY INQUIRIES ARE FROM IRRESPONSIBLE

3 Point on 6

PHOTOGRAPHERS HAVE AT LAST FOUND WAYS AND MEANS TO DRAMATIZE INDUSTRIAL SCENES AS

18 Point Copperplate

AND THIS IS THE

18 Point Small Caps

ONE OUT OF 67 OR

12 Point

THE SHEER MAGNITUDE

10 Point on 12

THE ADVERTISING MAN SHOWS

8 Point on 12

IF BOTH UNDERSTOOD THE REAL FACTS

6 Point

FOR EVERY NATIONAL ADVERTISING MANUFACTURER

5 Point on 6

I DO NOT EVEN DARE TO ATTEMPT TO FORECAST HOW LONG IT

4 Point on 6

NOT UNTIL YOU HAVE WITNESSED AN EXHIBITION, A COLLECTION OF THOUSANDS

61

30 Light Grot No. 8

SCENERY
beautify &
makes the

48 Heavy Grot No. 6.

OWE
debts

24 Point

A HISTORIC
border town
in the heart

36 Point

TOWNS
12 great

18 Point

THE MODE OF
travelling in the
country is far

24 Point

EXCEPTED
candidate &

12 Point

THE FAME OF RURAL
Britain has gone around
the world, and for many

18 Point

EXCURSIONS
to any part of

10 Point

HISTORY HAS LEFT THE
romantic glamour over nearly
all the land in the form of
the modern and up-to-date

12 Point

GREAT BRITAIN IS
always a magnetic

8 Point

THESE AND MANY MORE RELICS
of bygone ages, in a setting of con-
stantly varying scenery, make the
joy of sightseeing a continued
interesting subject for visitors who

10 Point

LONDON IS THE POINT
from which to make an

8 Point

THE MANY MUSEUMS ARE
a fund of interest and enjoyment to a perennial flow of

6 Point

THERE ARE CERTAIN FEATURES OF THE
country landscape, the century-old hedges,
the charming gardens and country houses,
and quaint old inns, with their reputation
for solid comfort that are so peculiar,
that some of the visitors come over to

6 Point

THE ANCIENT UNIVERSITIES OF
Oxford and Cambridge rival the
capital in interest and in fame.

62

BARTLETT

60 Point

MAKES many of the

48 Point

A GOOD & very profitable

36 Point

PRICE! The £24

24 Point

A VERY easy thing invariably

18 Point

THE SMALL initial cost of the insurance is such as to render the

12 Point

NO MATTER WHAT poor printing costs, it is not worth what you pay for it. Poor printing, small

10 Point

POOR PRINTING COSTS just as much to address and as much for postage as Good Printing, and when judged by the number and quality of the

8 Point

EVERY MANUFACTURER HAS a sales problem. To him this problem appears very difficult, possibly almost without any solution. In reality, his problem is very simple. To illustrate concretely, here is a manufacturer of

6 Point

ALL ADVERTISING IS BASED ON something written—then circulated. This circulation may be by newspaper or by periodical, letter, booklet or other mediums. It is important to remember that advertising is not mediums, but words. Mediums simply multiply the original draft or idea.

63

AUTHOR'S ROMAN

14 Point

THE ADVERTISER of to-day is not fully aware of the many possibilities before him of creating to the best

12 Point

THIS STYLE HAS COME very largely into use and has strongly influenced the developments of other and later methods of display, but nevertheless, when it

10 Point

THE BEST OF THE ORIGINAL fancy borderings have survived up to the present day and, in addition, we have an unlimited array of modern ornament from which to draw. With regard to the many and interchangeable

10 Point Italic

THE FIRST & FOREMOST necessity should be that of a standard. Without a definite understanding that a standard creates, there can be no real measurement of work. There is no estimating the real and

8 Point

PRINTING IS IN MUCH ABOUT THE same condition as the periodicals — under their hand is a potential field of such infinitely vast proportions that present business, large as it is, would look very diminutive as compared to it. This business will continue to remain the same until it is visualised by

6 Point

THE SUCCESSFUL DESIGNER MUST KEEP himself conversant with the current work of the day. He should carefully take notice of the materials used in up-to-date printing offices, and the special methods of gaining the results obtained. A good designer is a man of ready resource and capable of making the most of the material with which he has to work with. It is futile for the designer to

48 Point

SOME 32 and

36 Point

CAN BE used still

30 Point

IT IS AN advantage to know &

24 Point

PERHAPS IT is not without significance that many of

18 Point

IT CANNOT BE too often pointed that a book falls within the domain of art, because it

64

CUSHING and GOTHIC

24 Point Cushing

STAINING—
which is one
of the initial

18 Point

**BEFORE GOING
into frames, the
lumber passes
through different**

14 Point

**EXPANSION AND
contraction are then
reduced to a point
that means practical
permanence of the**

12 Point

**OAK COMPRISES A
fair proportion of all wood
used in furniture making.
Heavy, hard, strong and
tough, it scores high in
wearing qualities.   Oak is**

10 Point

QUARTERED OAK IS A TERM
applied to lumber obtained from
cutting a log as near as possible
parallel to the medullary rays,
which extend outward from the
heart of the log like spokes from
the hub of a wheel. The saw,

8 Point

THE DIFFERENCE BETWEEN GOOD
and poor lumber is in the time given
it to dry and the care with which the
next operation, kiln drying, is done.
Simply, a kiln is a room provided with
(1) a means of supplying heat at the
bottom to circulate up through the
lumber, piled crosswise on trucks above

48 Point

OAK &
walnut

36 Point

WHEN A
huge tree

36 Point Gothic

MANY
of the

30 Point

IF THIS
wood is

24 Point

MAPLE IS
similar in
grain and

18 Point

**ON A CROSS
section piece
the pores will
be found very**

65

FLEMISH BLACK

72 Point

In the Old Days only

60 Point

Not until the Year 1697 &

48 Point

When it featured several

42 Point

Here is a naturally designed

30 Point

During this Period, many changes took

24 Point

Several designs in vogue during that century are

18 Point

It characterised the ideals maintained at the beginning of the era, when so many

ABBEY TEXT

2 Line Pica

This Period
saw the com=
plete change
from the very

Great Primer

Ideals of comfort
and convenience
began to exert a
stronger influence
during the era of

Pica

The Queen Anne style
marked the ascendency of
the curve over the straight
line, and also the trend
toward lighter and more
graceful designs. There

Long Primer

The qualities of grace and
refinement introduced during
this period were perpetuated
by Sheraton in more sub=
stantial form. Sheraton's
chairs were his most striking
articles. The ornamentation

Brevier

During the reign of Louis XV, French
Court life was characterized by ease,
luxury and splendour. Furniture re=
flected that life; in it the passion for
curves was carried to the point of
delirium and straight, structural lines
seldom appeared. Very elaborate in
every detail, and considered more

5 Line Pica

Many
of the

4 Line Pica

In 1872
styles &

3 Line Pica

Jacobean
furniture
was quite

2 Line Great Primer

The Dutch
influence is
very strong
in this style

67

INITIALS

96 Point Cloister

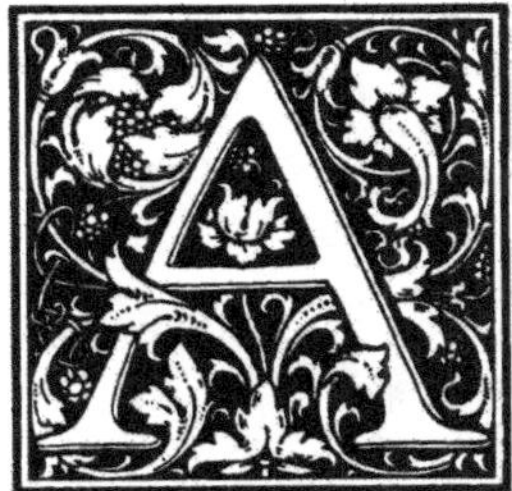 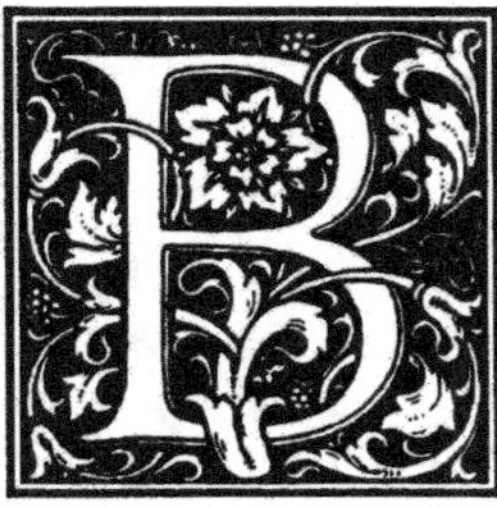 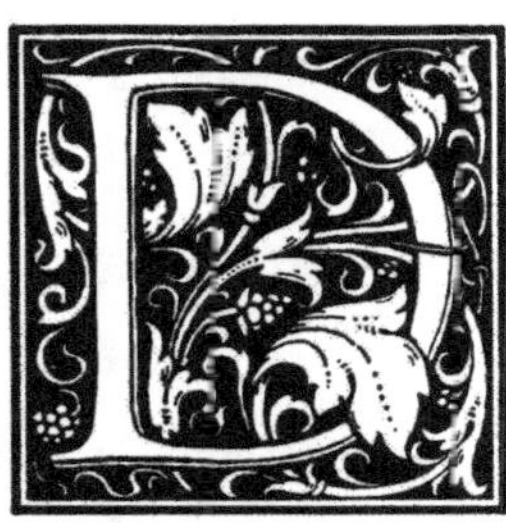

120 Point Versatile

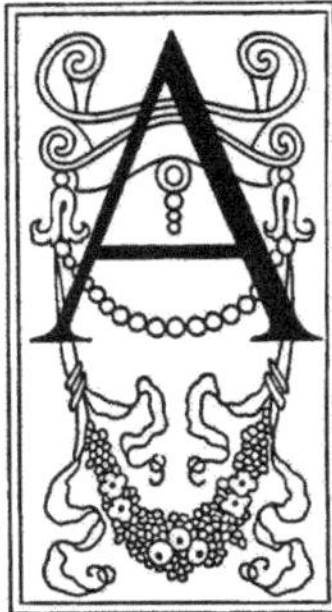 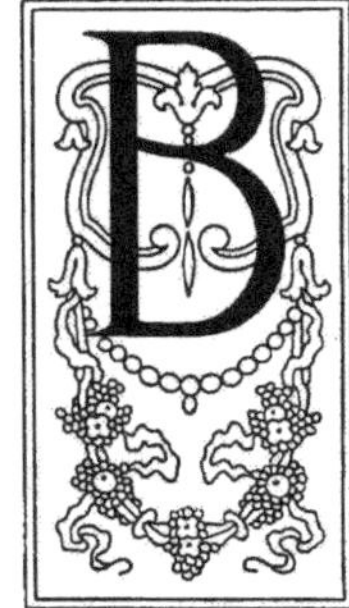 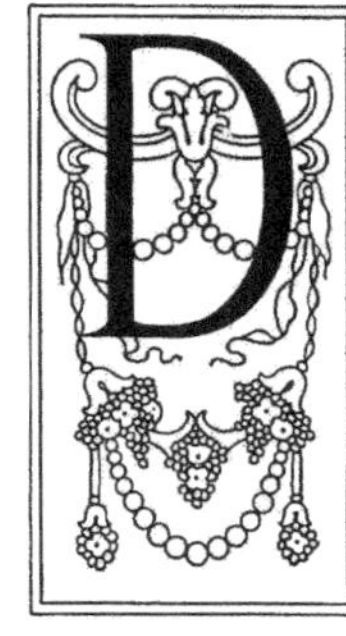 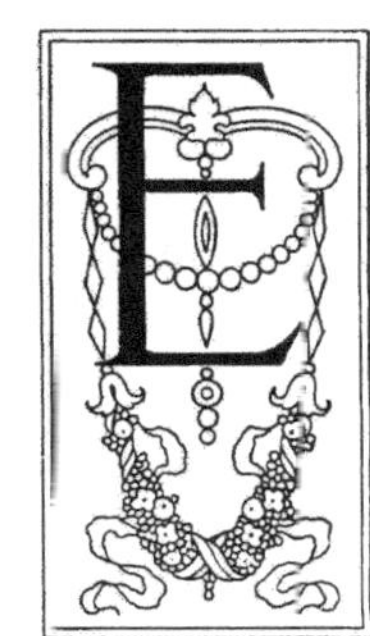

72 Point Bodoni Shaded (2 Colours)

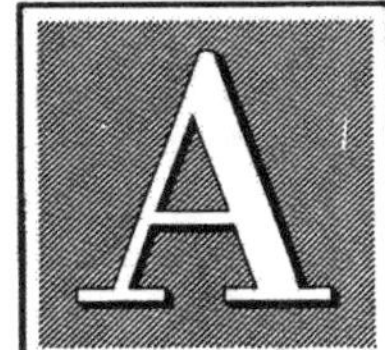 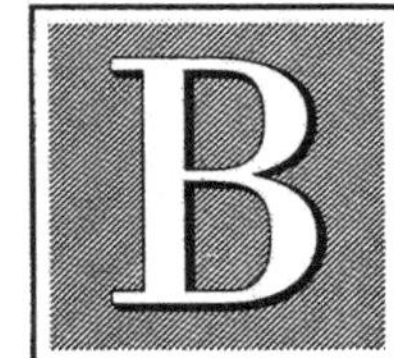

48 Point Bodoni Shaded (2 Colours)

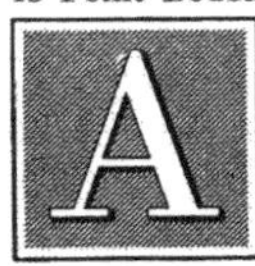 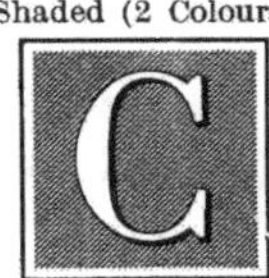 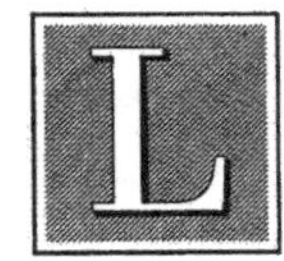

36 Point Bodoni Shaded (2 Colours)

 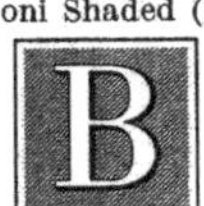 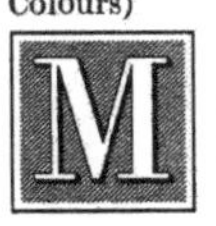 

48 Point Clearcut Shaded

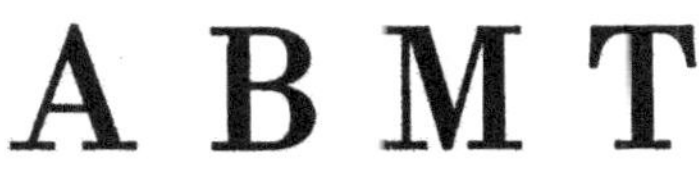 

36 Point Clearcut Shaded

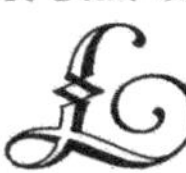 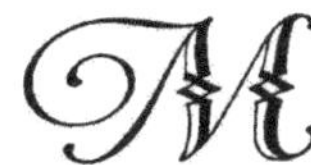   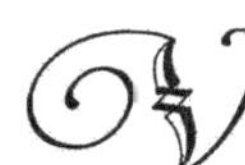

30 Point Clearcut Shaded

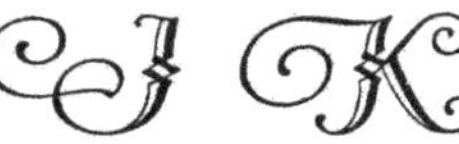 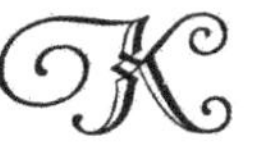 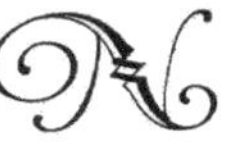 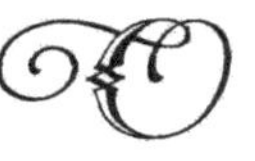 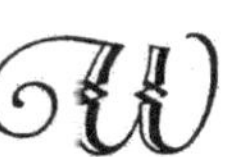 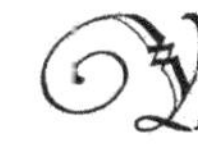

24 Point Clearcut Shaded

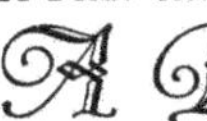 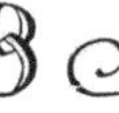 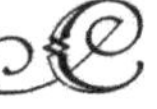 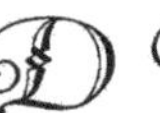 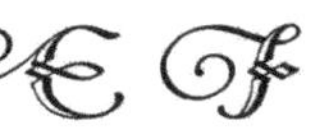 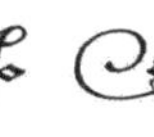 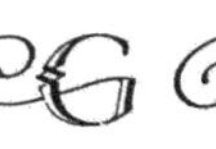 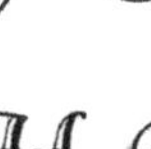 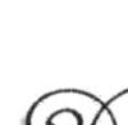

JAQUISH BORDER, OLD FASHIONED BORDER
ENGRAVERS' BORDER, HADDON BORDER, SWASTIKA BORDER

Jaquish No. 1	Jaquish No. 2	Old Fashioned. No. 13	Engravers No. 1201	Haddon No. 35	Swastika 12 Point	Swastika 6 Point

EPOCH and HARTWICK BORDERS

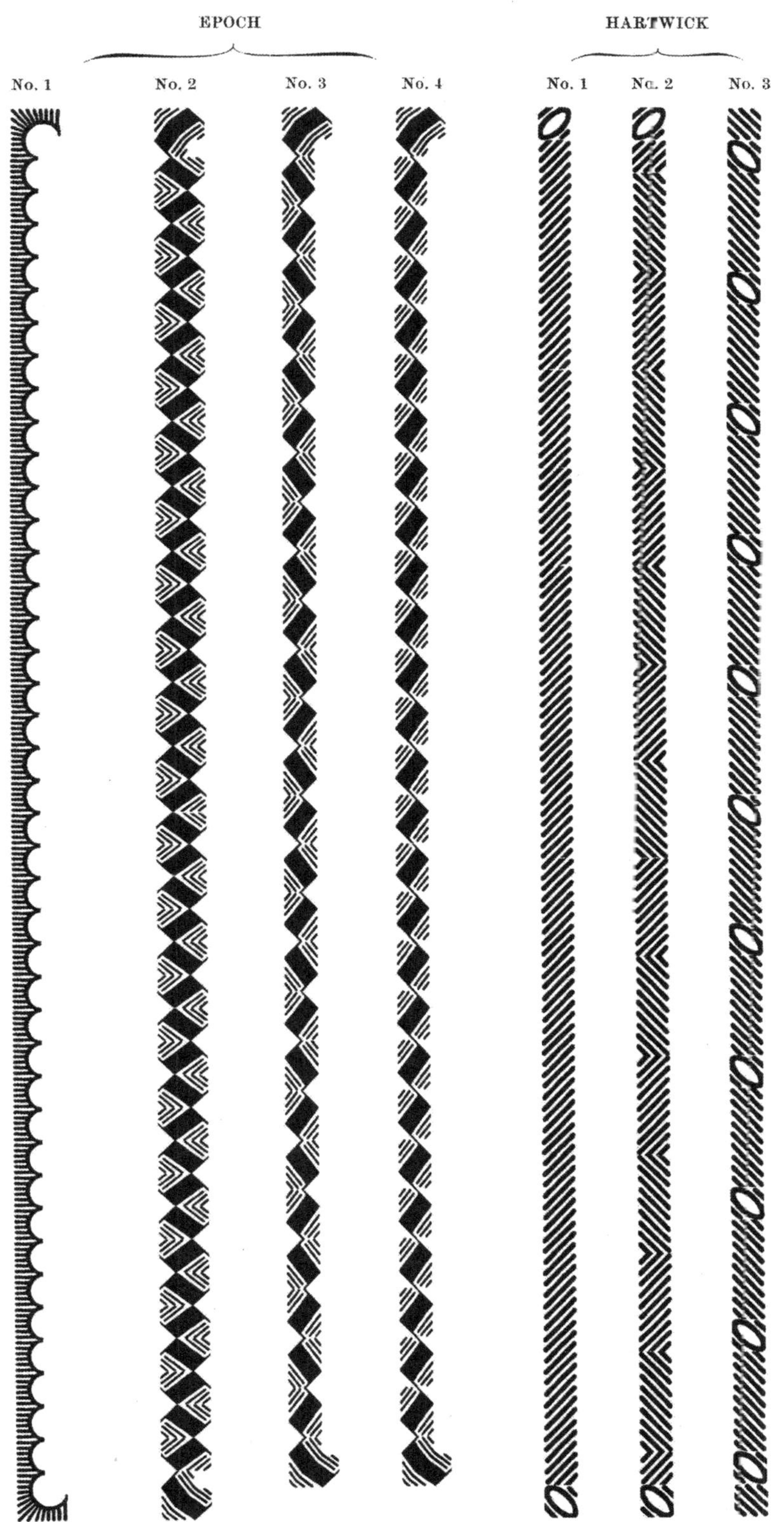

HAFTEL BORDER, GRECIAN BORDER
HOLLY BORDER, ZEBRA BORDER

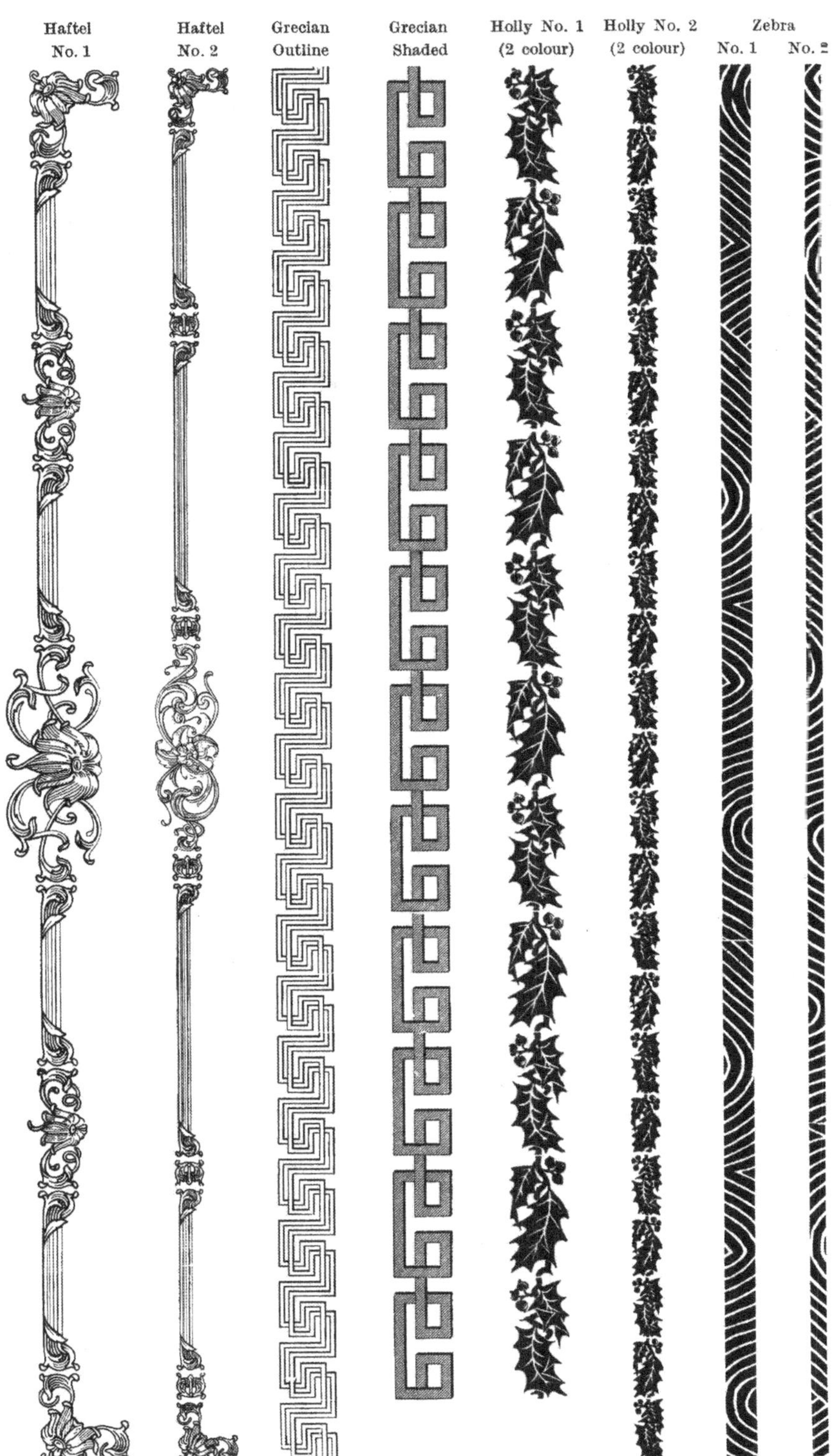

KLINGSPOR and ROSA BORDERS

Klingspor Borders

| 12 Point No. 17710 | 8 Point No. 17707 | 8 Point No. 16985 | 10 Point No. 16408 |

Rosa Borders

| 18 Point No. 2 | 18 Point No. 5 | 18 Point No. 10 |

MONO BORDERS

No. 1 No. 8 No. 17 No. 18 No. 20 No. 21 No. 23 No. 24 No. 25

MONO BORDERS

No. 4   No. 15   No. 16   No. 16a   No. 19   No. 19a   No. 29

MONO BORDERS

No. 30 No. 31 No. 32 No. 33 No. 34 No. 35 No. 36 No. 37

MONO BORDERS

No. 38   No. 39   No. 40   No. 41   No. 42   No. 43   No. 44   No. 45

MONO BORDERS

No. 46 No. 47 No. 48 No. 49 No. 50 No. 51 No. 52 No. 53

OVOLO BORDER, CHECK BORDER, SCHRAFFUR BORDER

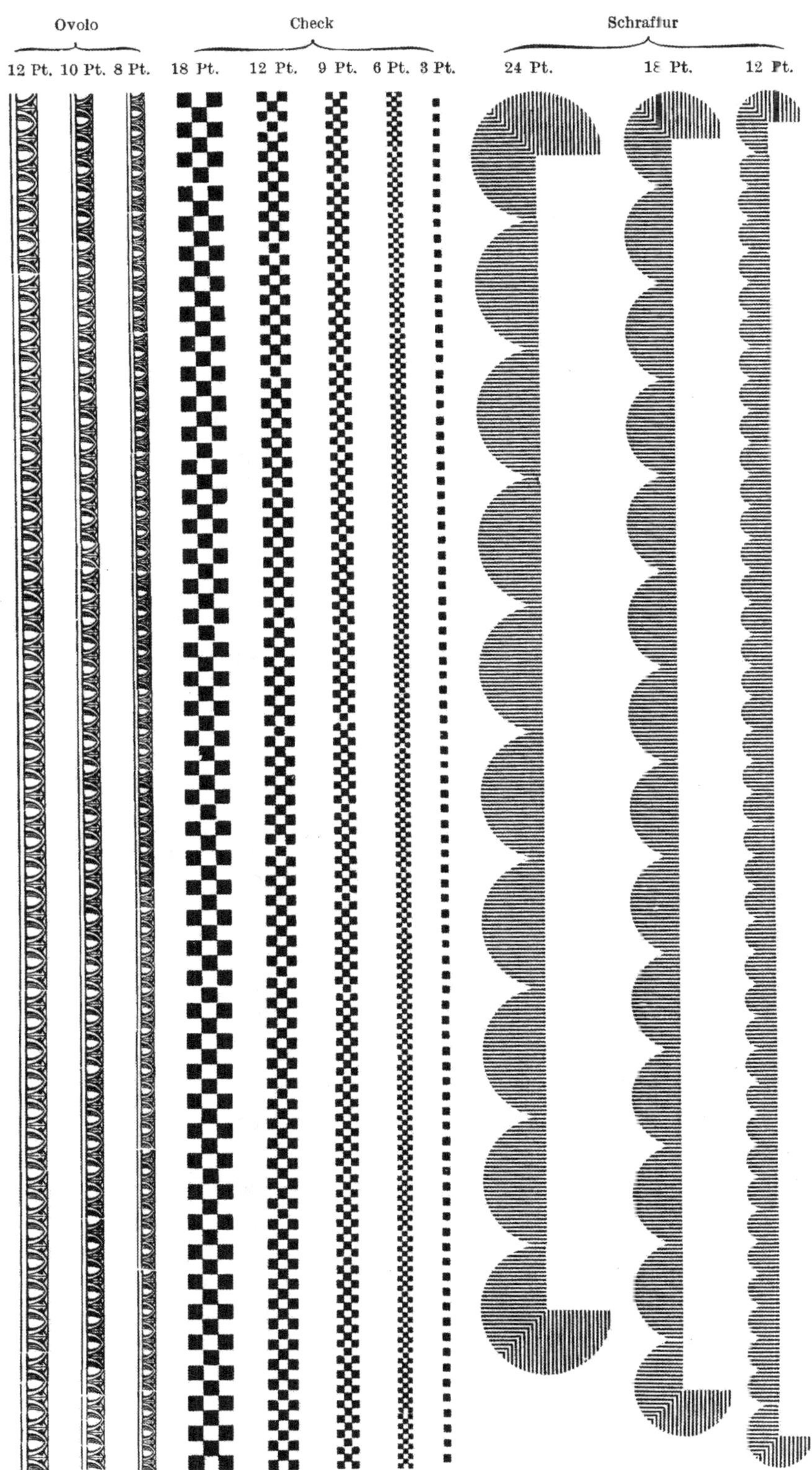

RANSOM BORDERS

8 Point	8 Point	10 Point	10 Point	12 Point	12 Point	18 Point	18 Point
No. 814	No. 815	No. 1003	No. 1004	No. 1447	No. 1448	No. 1967	No. 1968

TEAGUE BORDERS

| 3 Point | 6 Point | 6 Point | 12 Point | 12 Point | 12 Point | 12 Point | 12 Point | 6 Point |
| No. 322 | No. 617 | No. 618 | No. 1204 | No. 1205 | No. 1211 | No. 1212 | No. 1213 | No. 620 |

RULES

24 Point Solid

18 Point Solid

12 Point Solid

10 Point Solid

8 Point Solid

6 Point Solid

4 Point Solid

3 Point Solid

2 Point Solid

1½ Point Solid

Medium

Fine

12 Point Treble

10 Point Treble

8 Point Treble

6 Point Treble

4 Point Treble

3 Point Treble

12 Point Contrast

10 Point Contrast

8 Point Contrast

7 Point Contrast

6 Point Contrast

5 Point Contrast

4 Point Contrast

6 Point Thick and Thin

4 Point Thick and Thin

6 Point Double Thick

4 Point Double Thick

4 Point Double Medium

3 Point Double Medium

6 Point Heavy Wave

3 Point Heavy Wave

3 Point Wave

2 Point Wave

81

SHADED RULE, KODAK RULE, DOTTED RULE

24 Point Shaded Rule

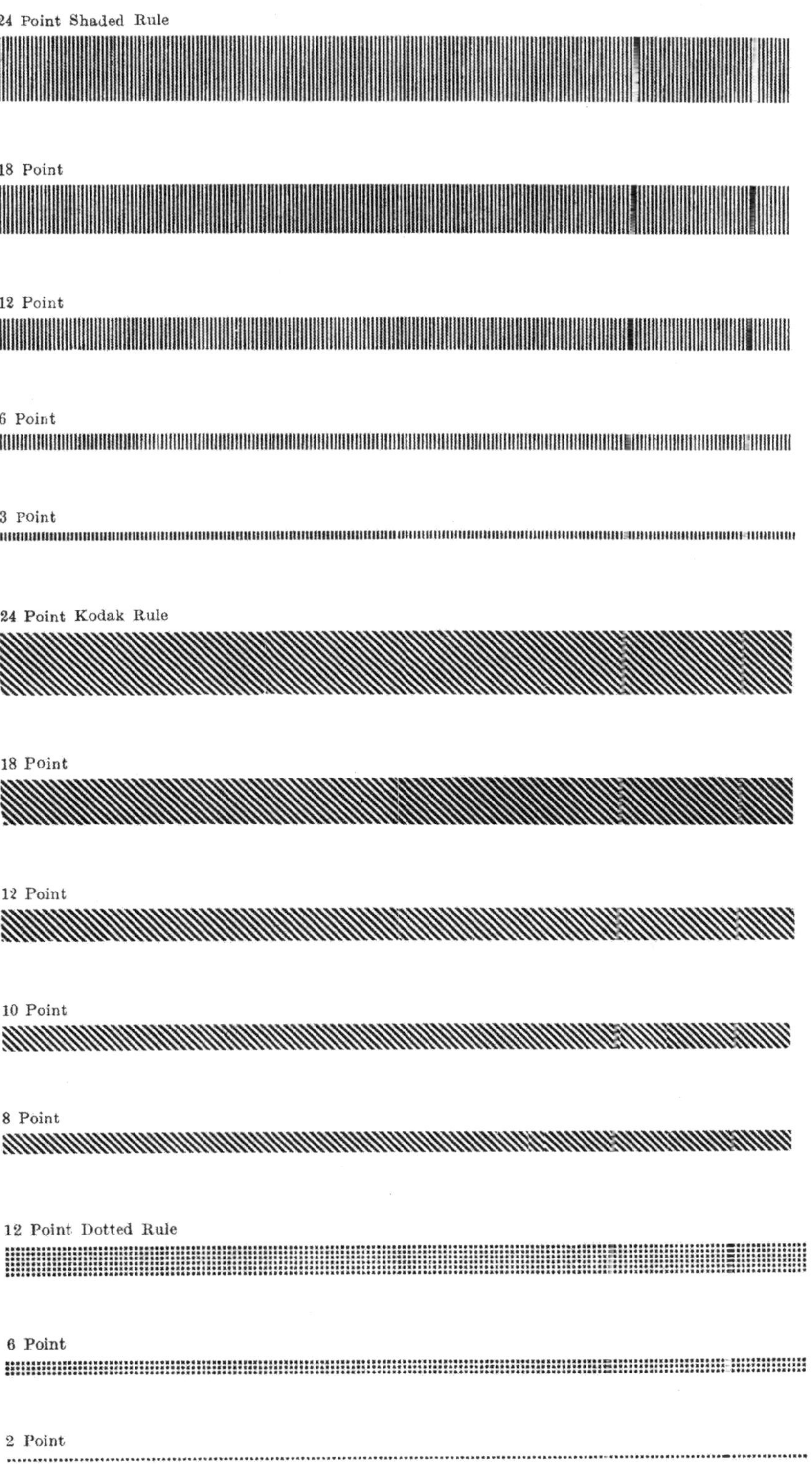

18 Point

12 Point

6 Point

3 Point

24 Point Kodak Rule

18 Point

12 Point

10 Point

8 Point

12 Point Dotted Rule

6 Point

2 Point

ADVERTISING BRACKETS

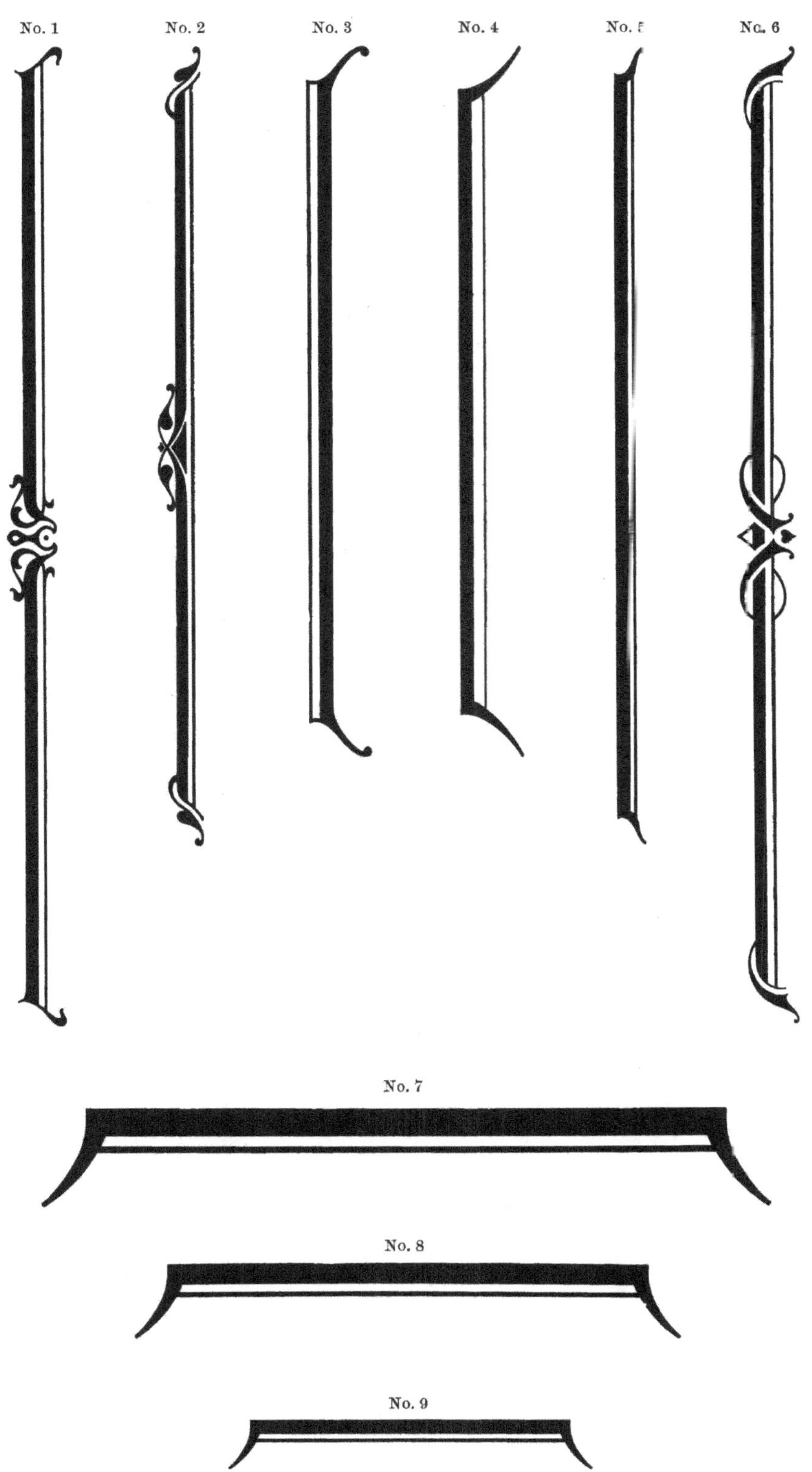

ADVERTISING BRACKETS

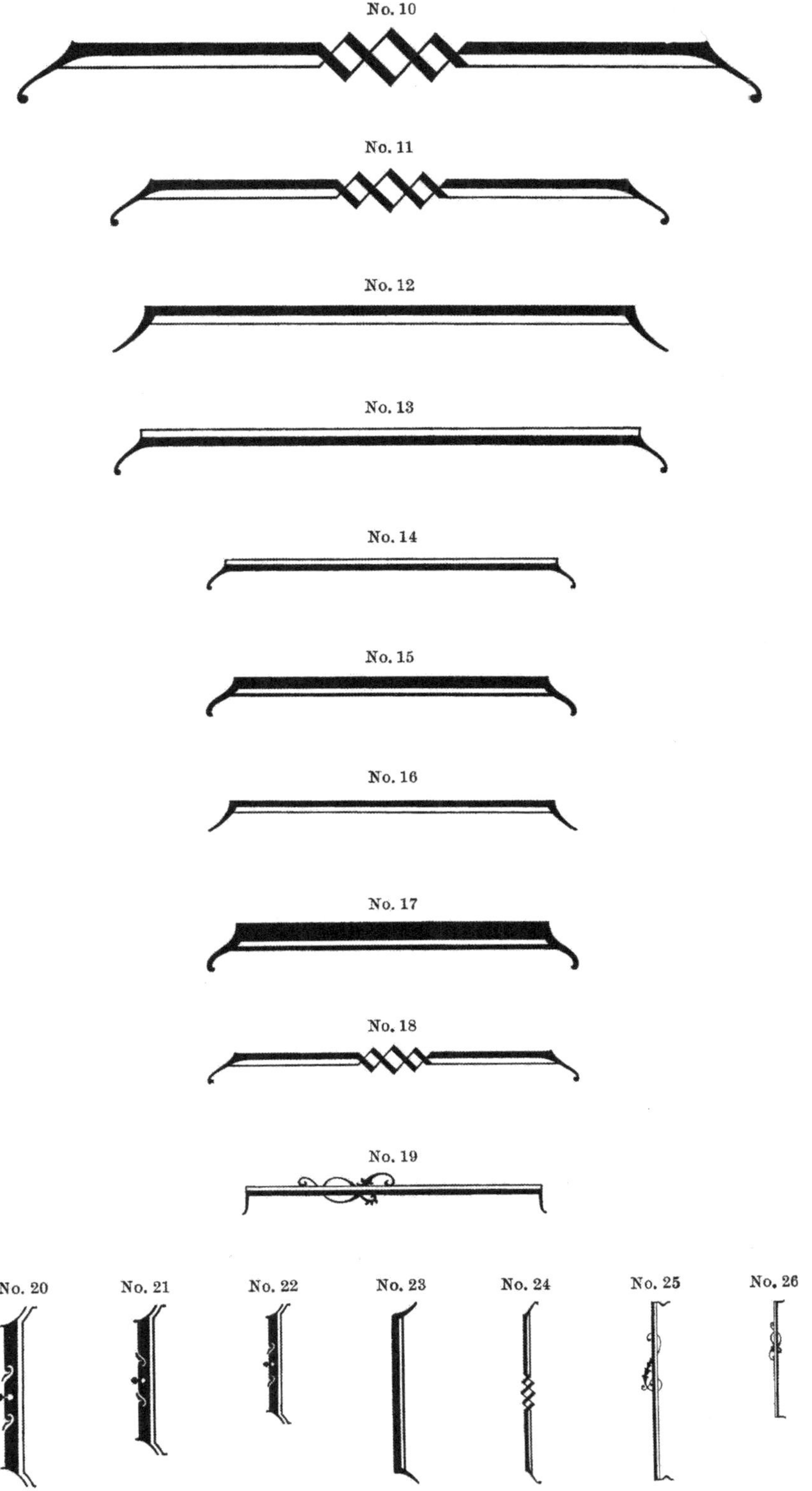